THE SOCIAL TEACHING
OF THE CHURCH

The Social Teaching of the Church

The Social Service Lecture, 1930

By

W. R. INGE, D.D., K.C.V.O.
Dean of St. Paul's Cathedral

WIPF & STOCK · Eugene, Oregon

Wipf and Stock Publishers
199 W 8th Ave, Suite 3
Eugene, OR 97401

The Social Teaching of the Church
The Social Service Lecture, 1930
By Inge, William R.
Copyright©1930 Methodist Publishing - Epworth Press
ISBN 13: 978-1-5326-3058-3
Publication date 4/5/2017
Previously published by Epworth Press, 1930

CONTENTS

PREFATORY NOTE

PREFATORY NOTE

I HAVE in the press a book called *Christian Ethics and Modern Problems,* which Messrs. Hodder and Stoughton will publish in the autumn. One chapter, as might be expected, deals with the attitude which Christians ought to take up towards social and economic questions. In other words, that chapter covers almost the same ground as this Lecture. When I prepared this Lecture my manuscript had left my hands; but it has been simply impossible for me to avoid repeating the arguments, and even some of the illustrations, such as two quotations from Lactantius and Harnack, which I had so recently put together for this section of my book. I must apologize for these repetitions, which may cause me to be accused of indolence; but the conditions laid down by the founders of this Lecture limit the lecturer to the social aspects of the Christian faith, on which I had just expressed my views to the best of my ability. For a more comprehensive study of the whole question, I must refer my readers to my forthcoming volume.

W. R. INGE.

Deanery, St. Paul's.

1

STEPS TOWARDS SOCIAL BETTERMENT

The Social Teaching of the Church

I

STEPS TOWARDS SOCIAL BETTERMENT

It is quite natural and inevitable that Christians should seek to find in their religion a sanction and support for those political and social convictions which they have reached on other than religious grounds. We all believe that Christianity has the promise of this life, as well as of that which is to come. We pray every day that the kingdom of God may come, and that the will of God may be done, on earth as it is in heaven. We are no longer satisfied with that conception of religion which sees in it only a flight from the world of time and change to a resting-place in the bosom of the Eternal. We all believe that we were sent into the world to make it, in however small a degree, a better place for our sojourn in it. Otherwise, the old problem whether it would not have been better for the soul to have remained in the eternal and spiritual world, instead of soiling and clogging its wings by contact with the impurities of matter, could hardly receive a satisfactory answer. Our marching orders are, 'See that thou make all things according to the pattern shewed to thee in the mount.'

The Christian life, therefore, brings us into relation with social as well as individual duties. Our duty towards our neighbour consists not only in a right attitude of the will and affections towards those with whom we have social relations; it involves also a loyalty towards the ideal of a Christian society, and a conscientious desire to understand, and if possible to contribute something towards the solution of the very difficult problems which beset all who are working towards social betterment. Can our religion give us any practical help in dealing with these problems?

When we seek for guidance of this kind, we are faced at once with the question of authority. We wish to get some help from our religion in dealing with problems which we admit to be difficult. But from what source do we hope to find such guidance? Is our authority to be the teaching of Christ as recorded in the Gospels, or may we add the Epistles of St. Paul as of almost equal inspiration? Or are we to consider that the Church is in possession of spiritual gifts which make it an authoritative guide in all questions of moral conduct? If we accept this view of the inspired wisdom of the institutional

Church, are we to include not only the Great Church, the Church which calls itself Catholic, but national Churches, and those independent sects which, though comparatively small in numbers, have had, especially in relation to social questions, a vigorous life of their own? In this Lecture I shall try to give a brief sketch of the social teaching of the Church, or the Churches, in the past, beginning with the New Testament; not, however, from the merely historical point of view, but all the time in the hope of making a little clearer what kind of help we may reasonably expect to find in this sort of inquiry. For I cannot doubt that the authority, both of the Bible and of the Church, is often illegitimately invoked to support political and social opinions on which neither the Gospel nor the Church can justly be held to give any decisive verdict.

We have to remember that any social and political teaching which has come down to us as part of the Christian tradition, must be considered in its historical context. This applies, above all, to the New Testament, because whatever is found there is commonly regarded as absolutely authoritative. But it applies also to the social teaching of the early Church, of the middle ages, of the Reformation period, and even of the nineteenth century, and in our own generation.

At the same time, wherever the Gospel is truly preached, morality, whether public or private, must be made to rest on principles of absolute and unchanging validity. Christianity is a revelation of the character of God and of His will towards mankind. Circumstances change, and with them the application of eternal principles to local and temporal conditions; but it is part of the religious view of reality that all earthly things must be valued as they appear when set against an eternal and spiritual background. All that passes away, as Goethe said, is only a symbol. It derives its dignity and permanent importance from its relation to what does not change and pass. History must always be treated as deriving its significance from the superhistorical. It has even been said that only the permanent can change.

Let us turn our eyes for a few moments to the condition of Palestine at the time when Christ 'tabernacled' among men in Galilee. Galilee was the home of a well-educated, independent, and fairly prosperous peasantry, not of pure Jewish descent. They were free from the sacerdotal bigotry and intolerance of Jerusalem, the spiritual home of all those who first kill the prophets and then build their sepulchres. Jesus was not 'le bon sans-culotte'; He and His disciples were not 'proletarians'; nor was there ever a time when the Church had any resemblance to the Communist party. The common people of Galilee were pious in a simple fashion, cherishing apocalyptic dreams of a good time coming, when God would intervene to restore political independence to His people, and establish a Kingdom of God, very vaguely conceived, on earth. There were some fanatical patriots, the Zealots, among them; but they do not seem to have been much infected by the bitter hatred of the rich which has always been common among unsuccessful Jews.

Christ, it must be said quite clearly, preached a Gospel of spiritual redemption, not of social reform. This would be absolutely clear if it were not for the Gospel of St. Luke, from which Christian Socialists draw nearly all their favourite texts. St. Luke seems to have been a warm-hearted man, with generous sympathies for the poor; when we compare his version of our Lord's teaching with that of St. Matthew and St. Mark, we are obliged to conclude that we must make some allowance for this subjective element in his record of his Master's ministry. For instance, it is he who represents the Beatitudes as referring to external conditions and not to the internal state of the heart; it is he who, in the parable of Dives and Lazarus, seems to suggest that in the next world a crude compensation will be paid to redress the economic inequalities

2

of this present time. But even he tells the highly significant story of how our Lord, when appealed to to 'speak to my brother, that he divide the inheritance with me,' refused to adjudicate, on the ground that questions of distribution were not in His province. Even St. Luke gives no support whatever to the idea that Christ was a revolutionary or a socialist reformer.

This is the more remarkable when we remember that Christ deliberately placed Himself in the line of the prophets, and that denunciation of social abuses was common form among the Old Testament prophets. We have to consider the meaning of this difference, for it is likely to affect our whole view of the relation of Christianity to secular politics.

I shall not spend much time in discussing the very modern theory that Christ was an apocalyptist, who proclaimed the approaching advent of a supernatural cataclysm, which would bring the existing world-order to an abrupt end. This theory, which was popularized by Schweitzer, has now, I think and hope, shrunk to its just proportions. When it was first propounded, it was greedily accepted by all who disliked German Liberal Protestantism— by Frenchmen like Loisy, a lucid and acute critic who objected to theologians like Harnack, both because they were Germans, and because their scepticism did not go far enough. Loisy preferred a God who ' is never encountered in history ' ; he said that the critic acknowledges ' comme deux Christs,' the historical Jesus of Nazareth, to whom he does not ascribe much significance, and the object of the Church's worship. So Schweitzer holds that the moral teaching of the Gospels was only an ' Interimsethik,' a provisional rule of conduct valid only during the short period before the Kingdom of God should come.

I have several times given my reasons for rejecting this theory, which would really deprive the Gospels of all value for us as a moral guide. The warnings about ' the day of the Lord ' are part of the prophetic tradition. The disciples certainly expected something startling to happen in their lifetime; what our Lord believed, and actually taught, is uncertain. But apocalyptism was never central in His teaching, and when the Church was obliged to realize that ' the Lord delayeth His coming,' Messianism, which had never had much meaning for the Jewish Dispersion, and still less for the Gentiles, dropped off so easily that we cannot suppose that it was ever of vital importance. It is also difficult to associate the character of Jesus Christ, the sanest and wisest of all spiritual teachers, with such fantastic and (as the events proved) absolutely groundless anticipations. I shall, therefore, take the view which, until lately, was universally held, that the ethical teaching of the Gospels is of permanent and universal validity, though we must make allowance for the particular conditions of society at the time and place at which it was revealed to mankind.

Some disparagement of New Testament ethics can also be traced in Catholics who are not Modernists, but who practically put the Church above the historical Jesus; by many modern thinkers who are frankly in revolt against some parts of traditional Christian morality; and by those whose religion is a matter of forms, ceremonies, and sacraments, rather than of conduct. These are in the habit of speaking of 'mere morality,' as something lower and more pedestrian than the practice of 'worship.' I must dissociate myself from all these points of view.

Christ, as has been well said by Dr. Glover, came to earth, not to teach men that He is like God, but that God is like Himself. In other words, His revelation was that 'the all-great is the all-loving too'; that God is our Father, not at all like a capricious Oriental sultan, not at all like what many of the Hebrews had imagined about Yahveh. But this itself was a proclamation of a purely ethical religion. From within, out of the heart of man, proceeds all that can defile, and all that can exalt,

the character. Almost all that the ordinary man
and woman mean by religion is pronounced to be
indifferent. This again is in line with the noblest
teaching of the old prophets, and with the Psalms
as a whole; but it had never before been declared
in so uncompromising a form. ' Not every one that
saith unto Me, Lord, Lord, shall enter into the
Kingdom of Heaven, but he that doeth the will of
My Father who is in heaven.' The law of love is
only a part of the law of inwardness. There can
be no substitute for a genuine and unselfish affection
towards our fellow-men, nor for a love of God
which seldom thinks of reward and punishment.

It was a fundamentally ethical teaching, and yet
fundamentally different from the formal legalistic
ethics of the Scribes and Pharisees. He made light
of the violation of ceremonial rules, and was indignant with those who ' teach for doctrines the
commandments of men.' Hypocrisy, hard-hearted-
ness, and calculating worldliness were the three
cardinal sins which roused Him to anger. They
are sins against love, and against that simplicity
and single-heartedness, which, as He taught, is
essential to a good life.

Whenever He deals with worldly affairs, it is
easy to see that His attitude is determined by a quite
distinctive standard of values, which it is not hard
to understand, though it is terribly difficult to make

it the principle of our daily lives. The texts which make His attitude clear are among the best known in the Gospels. ' Be not anxious about the morrow, for the morrow shall take thought for the things of itself.' As for meat, drink, and clothing, ' your heavenly Father knoweth that ye have need of all these things.' ' Seek ye first the kingdom of God and His righteousness, and all these things shall be added unto you.' ' What is a man profited, if he shall gain the whole world and lose his own soul? ' ' No man can serve two masters; ye cannot serve God and Mammon.' ' If thine eye be single, thy whole body shall be full of light; but if thine eye be evil, thy whole body shall be full of darkness. If, therefore, the light that is in thee be darkness, how great is that darkness? ' And to the hoarder of money and goods, ' Thou fool, this night thy soul shall be required of thee.' There are many other texts to the same effect, and we can hardly miss their meaning. Christ sits very lightly to all the paraphernalia of life. He thinks that they are a clog and a hindrance to the spiritual life, and worth very little in themselves. ' Behold the lilies of the field. I say unto you that even Solomon in all his glory was not arrayed like one of these.' I have lately come from Palestine. The lilies were, I suppose, the scarlet anemones which, in the spring, carpet the fields, mingled with blue and purple flowers which grow in masses. Certainly no royal robes could vie with them in splendour and beauty. But how many poets and prophets before Wordsworth have seen this as simply and clearly as Christ did? He is not very indignant with the materialist who spends his life in getting and spending, 'laying waste his powers,' as Wordsworth says. He is not very indignant, but He is sorry for them, and thinks them silly. 'Thou fool,' not 'thou thief,' is what He says to the avaricious man.

All points in the same direction. The good things of this world do not make men happier or better, and if we devote ourselves to them they will make us unhappier and worse. This is not asceticism. Christ was not, in the ordinary sense, an ascetic. The hardships which He suffered were just the lot of an itinerant preacher, who must, by the way, have taken many long walks on rough and steep roads. His love of nature, especially of mountains, again reminds us of Wordsworth, who also lived very simply but not ascetically.

There are a few sayings about the danger of wealth which seem to go rather beyond what I have said. But there is no doubt that He used hyperbolical language, which can hardly be avoided in popular preaching. He did not shun the society of the rich, or repel them in any way. His counsel of perfection to the young man who thought that he had kept all the commandments was not addressed to everybody. In those days, perhaps, a man could hardly follow Christ in His journeys without giving up or endangering his hoarded wealth. There was no regular investment of capital in those days.

It is hardly necessary to say that even if He had wished to lay down a scheme of Socialism—and such an idea never occurred to Him—the conditions of Palestine under Pontius Pilate and Herod would have put it out of the question. He might have joined the Essenes, or founded a similar order of monks on communistic lines, but He never thought of doing so. His travelling missionaries were to live on alms, like begging friars; but this proves nothing. His own little band seem to have carried a 'bag' with money in it, and to have bought food when they needed it.

II
PROBLEMS OF DISTRIBUTION
AND CONSUMPTION

II

PROBLEMS OF DISTRIBUTION
AND CONSUMPTION

We must then come to the conclusion that the
Gospels have nothing to teach us about problems of
distribution. They will not decide for us whether
we ought to vote for Conservatives, Liberals, or
Socialists. But they have everything to teach us
about the relative importance which we ought to
attach to all that class of goods in which one man's
gain is another man's loss, in comparison with those
intellectual, artistic, and spiritual goods which are
increased by sharing them, and which cannot be
taken away from us, since they are part of our
personality. We may speculate, if we will, on the
political, economic, and social consequences which
would follow if a whole nation was converted to the
Christian standard of values. It seems probable
that the so-called social question would be found
to have solved itself.

There are some, I know, who think that the
Sermon on the Mount points directly to the fantastic doctrines of Tolstoy, and that the adoption
of such principles of conduct as are indicated by,

' give to him that asketh thee,' and ' resist not the evil man,' are manifestly incompatible with any system of private ownership. This, though it has been held by such able men as Prof. Percy Gardner, seems to me rather unintelligent literalism. Christ was a prophet, not a legislator; He gives us principles, not rules; we are meant to use common sense in interpreting them. To give one instance only. Christ enjoins us to turn the other cheek when we are smitten. But He Himself, when He was smitten, did not turn the other cheek, but administered a dignified rebuke to the smiter.

Some of us may be disappointed at being told that we can get no more definite guidance than this from the Gospels. On this I have two remarks to make. Some people reject Christianity because they do not understand it; others because they do understand it. To the latter class unquestionably belong the disciples of Karl Marx. For what excites their passionate hatred of Christianity is precisely that idealistic standard of values which cuts the ground from under the feet of their savage and vindictive materialism. I could easily prove from their writings, if it were worth while, that what infuriates them more than anything else is the doctrine of Christ about cleansing the inside of the cup, that the outside may be clean also. From within outwards; from the heart and will of the man to his outer life and conduct; from the moral individual to the society: that is unquestionably the teaching of Christ, and the very heart and kernel of His message. The Marxian doctrine is the exact opposite. Reform institutions, and mankind, who are naturally good, will behave like good citizens. Such was also the teaching of Rousseau, against which Carlyle protests in well-known and trenchant words. Here no compromise is possible. If Christ is right, Rousseau and Marx are utterly wrong. If Lenin and his disciples had turned Russia into an earthly paradise, we might have some qualms about the wisdom of the Christian method. At any rate, there must be internecine war between the two theories, as the Russian Communists fully recognize. I am far from thinking that Christianity is so invertebrate as to be compatible with every theory which may be honestly and sincerely held. In my opinion, there are some religions, some ethical theories, and some philosophies, which resist being Christianized.

That is one point on which I think we may say that the Gospel gives us definite guidance. The materialism of Marxian Socialism is ruled out. This issue is more clearly defined on the Continent than in our illogical country. The Roman Catholics understand it—no Catholic is allowed to be a Communist. On this point I shall have more to say presently, for it was not without some hesitation that the Church accepted the doctrine that the right to hold private property is part of the law of nature. It would, of course, be possible to deny this last statement, while at the same time rejecting the materialism of Marx. But the modern Communists have declared war against religion in any form. A whole series of declarations might be quoted, such as ' The first word of religion is a lie ' ; ' Religion is opium,' and many more of the same kind. It is quite a mistake to suppose that the campaign in Russia is directed only against the superstitious and largely unethical teaching and practices of the Orthodox Church.

In our own country, on the other hand, Christian Socialism is not felt to be a contradiction in terms. A cleavage exists between the Labour party, which includes many believing Christians, and the Communists, a comparatively small body which is actively anti-religious. The latter explicitly reject the Christian standard of values; the former profess to retain it, but in reality have so secularized their religion that it is no longer purely Christian. The same may, of course, be said of many Christians who belong to other parties, and especially to those comfortable people who think that they have made a working compromise between the service of God and that of Mammon. The

crucial question in every case is whether there is
any real conviction that the standard of values
which we find in the Gospels is the true one. The
over-estimate of the importance of money, and the
things which money will buy, may be as great
among those who wish to redistribute wealth as
among those who wish to maintain things as they
are.

The other point—I said there were two on which
I wished to speak—is one to which I attach great
importance. I ask you specially to attend to it,
because, while there is probably no difference of
opinion among those who hear me as to the contradiction   between   Christianity   and   Bolshevik
materialism, you may not all agree with me in what
I am now going to say.

We have seen that Christ pointedly declined to
act as arbitrator in a disputed question of ownership. He merely turned to His disciples with the
words, ' Take heed and beware of all covetousness,
for a man's life consisteth not in the abundance of
the things which he possesseth.' The Church has
to do with the motives and desires and passions
which lead to disputes about the distribution of
wealth.   It   condemns   the   irrational   love   of
accumulation. But we have no right to say that
one system of taxation is more Christian than
another. The Good Samaritan in the parable set

the wounded man on his own beast, and paid his hotel bill with his own money. The modern version of the parable seems to make him run after the priest and Levite, and take the horse of one and the purse of the other. But would not St. Paul have said, ' Though I give all my neighbours' goods to feed the poor, and have not charity, I am nothing ' ?

This, I think, may fairly be objected against some who talk about Christian politics and economics. Special taxation of large incomes may be desirable on public grounds, but it is no substitute for Christian love or charity, and cannot claim to be in accordance with ' Christian economics.' There is no Christian economics, but only a Christian and an unchristian way of approaching all such questions.

But (I am now coming to my second point) does our Lord leave us equally without definite guidance in questions of consumption? I maintain that here we shall really find something like definite principles. I also think that in books and treatises upon economics, and in all that is said and written on the subject in our time, too much attention is given to production and distribution, and not enough to consumption. I should even say that the way we spend our money is more important, as a public duty, than the way we acquire it. The homely maxim, ' waste not,' may be of more ethical importance than most of us think. All nations waste a good deal, the French much less than the English, the English much less than the Americans. In a recent book (the title is *Whither Mankind?*) the most amazing figures are given of the amount spent every year in the United States on different forms of sport and play. I will not trouble you with the items, startling as some of them are; but the upshot is that the American play-budget is rather larger that the aggregate income of all the citizens of the British Isles. The grand total is estimated at twenty-one thousand million dollars. Two years of American play would pay off our entire war debt.

Now I want you to consider what this prodigious expenditure on play means. I do not take the Puritanical view that all unnecessary recreation partakes of the nature of sin—far from it. But perhaps two thousand million on ' candy, chewing-gum, hard and soft drinks ' may be thought excessive, and two hundred and fifty million on ' phonographs, pianolas, &c.' a generous allowance. For all these indulgences represent some one's labour more or less thrown away. We often hear that the real grievance of the working man is not so much that he has to work too hard, or that he is poorly paid, as that so much of his labour is wasted, devoted to making things which nobody ought to want, and which a man can hardly give his time to making without some loss of self-respect. Well, whose fault is that? The fault of the employers? No, but the fault of the consumers. It is they who pay the piper and call the tune. It is they who condemn both employers and working men to waste their energies on frivolities which do no good to anybody. If the country is feeling the pinch of poverty, may not our wastefulness, though it is not so great as that of the Americans, be a prime cause?

Now here we are ' up against ' (to use a popular vulgarism) not only the practice of the richer nations, but against a theory which justifies it. I think it was the French Socialist, Fourier, who said that the ideal is to increase every one's wants and the means of gratifying them. Marx and Lassalle complained of the ' verdammte Bedurfnisslosigkeit ' —the accursed paucity of wants—which prevents the masses from being as discontented as they wished to make them. In America there is a very popular economic theory which they call ' consumptionism.' Let every one form as many new tastes— the same tastes if possible—as he can. Then he will want to buy more things every year. This will be good for trade, and will stimulate massproduction, which is very profitable. Mass-production makes it possible to pay very high wages, which are all spent in gratifying the new wants. So production and consumption play into each other's hands. The money circulates briskly; the figures of trade go up year by year. All the citizens perform a patriotic duty by earning and spending as much as possible. Hence the national play bill of twenty-one thousand million dollars; hence the colossal fortunes of Henry Ford and Woolworth. Everybody is happy, or would be if he gave himself time to think. But with work and play provided for every hour in the day, why should he be bothered to think? Thinking is hard work, and not always conducive to unqualified optimism.

Well, we probably do not think the result very satisfactory. If we were sent into the world to live in this way, it was hardly worth while to create our precious species to exterminate all the other animals, to deface the surface of the planet, and squander in a century natural resources which took tens of thousands of years to store up. And it does seem to me that this ideal is not only vulgar and uncivilized, but contrary to the ethics of the New Testament.

There is a good deal, both in the Gospels and in St. Paul's Epistles, bearing on the ethics of consumption. 'Having food and raiment, let us be therewith content,' is one of the clearest statements. But without giving a string of texts detached from their context, may we not say that the whole tone of the New Testament is in favour of a simple life of steady but not feverish industry, not entirely crowded up with work or play, but leaving an ample margin for those unhurried occupations which make family life enjoyable, and allow us, in Matthew Arnold's words, to possess our souls before we die?

You see, then, that I am advocating a fairly simple and not too crowded life as being that which Christ and His disciples would recommend as most favourable to spiritual progress. I put it primarily on religious grounds. The life of a good man is a life of prayer, by which I do not mean only or chiefly petition, but communion with God, elevation of the mind to God, meditation on holy and serious subjects, recollection, to use a good old word. This is precisely the kind of life which modern conditions make it difficult to lead. Men and women get so much out of the habit of thinking quietly, of trying to know themselves, the world around them, and the God who is both above us, around us, and within us, that the highest faculties of the soul rust and atrophy from disuse, and we live as strangers to all the higher values. 'Thou fool, this night they are demanding thy soul.' My soul; what have I done with it? Have I got a soul any longer?

To descend from this to a slightly lower plane. Critics from the Latin nations, like George Santayana and Madariaga, both men of Spanish extraction who know the Anglo-Saxon countries well, think that we and the Americans are only half civilized because we have given so little thought to get our values right. Matthew Arnold, as we know, became almost a bore by constantly repeating the same thing. He wanted us to be more Greek and less Hebraic. ' Take heed that the light that is in thee be not darkness.' We need not separate religion from other spiritual values; they are all part of the higher life; and Wordsworth was not the first to teach us that plain living and high thinking go together, or at least that high living is an obstacle to high thinking. This, and not a sense of injustice, is, I think, at the bottom of our Lord's warnings against the deceitfulness of riches and the cares of life, which choke the word so that it becometh unfruitful.

III
THE ATTITUDE OF THE
NEW TESTAMENT

III
THE ATTITUDE OF THE NEW TESTAMENT

THIS then, so far as I could express my meaning in a few pages of manuscript, is the attitude of the New Testament towards the social question. Christianity, as I have said elsewhere, is a revolutionary idealism, which estranges revolutionaries because it is idealistic, and conservatives because it is revolutionary. It is a revaluation of all values, which demonetizes the world's currency, and offers rewards which the worldling does not want. 'Peace I leave with you, My peace I give unto you; not as the world giveth, give I unto you.' That is the crux of the whole business. The Churches have tried to work by bribes and threats —essentially irreligious appeals to attract or terrify the irreligious. These methods have failed, and we talk of the decay of religion. The real appeal of Christ is as strong as ever; but we are nowhere led to expect that there will ever be an inconvenient crowd trying to enter by the narrow gate.

The Christian standard of values is permanently

true. But I should not be honest if I suppressed my conviction that there is something lacking both in the outlook of the New Testament and in that of the Church, both in early times and down to our own day. 'The rapture of the forward view,' as George Meredith puts it, was wanting under the Roman empire. The Jews certainly looked for an ultimate triumph of the right cause, to be achieved in history. 'The Lord is a man of war; the Lord of hosts is His name.' The time would come when Israel should bruise its oppressors with a rod of iron, and break them in pieces like a potter's vessel. But for a long time the political prospects of the little nation had been so hopeless that the indomitable optimism of the worshippers of Yahveh had come to rest on dreams of a purely supernatural deliverance. The nation had become a Church, and patriotism had become apocalyptic. The idea of a national recovery by human effort had died down. In the Gentile world there was a similar absence of political aspiration. The Roman steam-roller had obliterated the turbulent ambitions of the Greek city states. Plato's Republic had taken wings and flown to an ideal world beyond space and time. 'Let us flee hence to our dear country'; and the dear country was nowhere on earth. At the time when Christianity triumphed over the sporadic persecutions of the imperial government, a deep pessimism had invaded the empire. Population was waning; even the soil, it was thought, was exhausted; the line of defence which protected civilization against barbarism had been pierced again and again. The notion of an 'end of the age,' a legacy of Palestinian apocalyptism, helped to paralyse the secular energies of the Christian Church, and infected even the Pagans. In short, we look in vain for any trace of that inspiring vision of a better world, to be brought about on this earth by the collective efforts of mankind, which forms so large a part of the idealism of our own time.

The result of this despair of civilization is to be found in the strange passion for flight from the world, which fills a large chapter in Church history. It seemed no great sacrifice to flee from a society such as that of the later Western empire, groaning under a rapacious despotism. So the cult of asceticism, of the 'religious' life of the monks and hermits, grew and spread, till the deserts were full of holy men and women, macerating their bodies, and turning in horror from the idea of marriage.

Since our subject is the social teaching of the Church, it is worth while to notice that here and here only we find a successful attempt to put Communism into practice. The chapter in the Acts of the Apostles about the little society of Christians at Jerusalem, who 'had all things common,' has been made too much of. It was not an experiment in Communism, but a voluntary sharing of goods by a band of enthusiasts brimming over with 'love of the brethren.' During the persecutions, when a severe weeding out of the half-hearted made the Church purer than it ever was later, the organization of the Church on the social side resembled that of a benefit society with very liberal management. The sick and aged and unfortunate were cared for at the expense of the community; but idleness was sternly discouraged. The spirit of brotherhood was still very strong.

But the monasteries were real experiments in Communism. History seems to have proved that such experiments can succeed only under two conditions—a religious basis and a rule of celibacy. Even so, the collective wealth of the community often proved a snare. There was a sect of Communists in America who bought land under which minerals were found. They ceased to fill vacancies, and formed themselves into a tontine. The last Communist was a very aged and childless millionaire. But there have been, and probably always will be, many persons of both sexes who are glad to be relieved from all necessity of thinking about the means of livelihood. Communal life was made for such persons, and it is a loss to Protestant countries to have so little provision for these tastes.

During the Christian Socialist Movement towards the end of the last century, certain clergymen collected and published extracts from the Fathers of the Church, which breathed a spirit of antagonism against private property. It is true that such utterances can be found, and that they become more violent after the victory of the Church. But it would be a mistake to suppose that they indicate any disposition on the part of the Church to take part in a class warfare. In the New Testament there is no trace of such a thing except in the most Jewish book of the New Testament, the Epistle of James, in which we find echoes of that class-hatred which is prominent in the Jewish literature of the time. But the ' rich ' who are there denounced are members of the Church. Some of the Christian Fathers, such as Ambrose, were much influenced by the later Stoicism, which was really a revival of Cynicism, and we see from Seneca, who was a millionaire, that the Stoics were prone to rather rhetorical language about luxury and wealth. The desire to reduce our wants to a minimum in order to be independent of fortune was a large part of the later philosophy, and in a sane and moderate form it may claim to be Christian. This is rather different from ' la propriété c'est le vol,' which was not really held by the Christian Fathers, in spite of a few rhetorical expressions which seem to imply it. I think Troeltsch is right when he says that ' the ruling principle in the praise of poverty is not the hoped-for downfall of the rich, but the ascetic-religious trend of thought, which is the opposite of Socialism.' It has long caused me amusement to see a wealthy congregation singing the Magnificat, which is much more violent than the ' Red Flag.' It shows how little we can rely on liturgical forms as indicating the real beliefs of those who use them. It seems certain that though the early Church was freely accused of want of patriotism, and of indifference to the fate of civilization, its enemies could never pretend that it was a dangerous revolutionary society. In spite of severe provocation, the Christians never agitated against the imperial government.

The dignity of work was not sufficiently recognized in the early Church. Here we may trace the influence of Genesis iii, but also the disparagement of manual labour which is inseparable from the institution of slavery. Hence we do not find the *uselessness* of the ascetic life urged against it. In a world without aspirations for the future the almost universal desire to leave children to carry on our name and continue our work was nearly quenched.

It is broadly true to say that at least until Augustine Christian ethics were mainly Stoical, Christian metaphysics Neoplatonic. Stoical influence by no means ceased with Augustine, but was revived much later in Calvinism, which is simply the Christian form of Stoicism. It is, therefore important to recognize how much influence the Stoical law of nature had upon Christian thought. Now the Stoical jurists were themselves not consistent or unanimous about the contents of the law of nature, especially as regards private property. The theory generally accepted by Catholic writers was that in a state of innocence there would be no private ownership; but that, besides the absolute law of nature which favoured Communism, there is a relative law of nature adapted to man's fallen state; and that in this fallen state private property is sanctioned by the relative law of nature under which we live. Private property is therefore recognized, and to deny the right to hold it is erroneous; but in a higher state of existence this would not be so. Undoubtedly this theory made men think that the communal life of the monasteries was a higher ideal than that of secular society.

But how did the Church interpret the Stoical maxim, so much in accordance with Christian teaching, that 'all men are by nature equal'?

The answer may be given in a quotation from
Lactantius, which fairly represents the view
accepted by the Church. ' Some one will say, Are
there not among you some poor, some rich, some
slaves, others masters?   Are these all differences
among individuals?   There is no other reason why
we call each other brothers, except that we believe
that we are all equal.   For since we measure all
human things by the spirit and not by the body,
although there are differences in bodily condition,
yet there are no slaves among us, but we count them
and call them our spiritual brethren, our fellow-
slaves in religion.   Riches also do not confer
distinction among us, except that they give the
opportunity of being more conspicuous in good
works.   Whereas, then, free men are equal in
humility with slaves, and rich with poor, in the
sight of God, we are distinguished according to
our virtues; the juster a man is, the higher his
rank.   If he bears himself not only as an equal but
as an inferior, he will receive a much higher dignity
in the judgement of God.   For in this earthly life
all things are short-lived and fugitive.'   That is to
say, all Christians are entitled to equal considera-
tion, without regard to their status in society; but
differences in worldly position are of so little
importance in the sight of God, that they should be
accepted as part of the secular order of things.

Thus Christian idealism has usually been a conservative force; but not always. It may easily be so applied as to have radical and even revolutionary consequences. We shall see that this has occasionally happened.

To pass on to the middle ages. We shall not find the modern idea of a Christian civilization in Thomas Aquinas any more than in the early Fathers. I will quote from the French writer, Feugueray, who sums up the radical difference between Thomist and modern social ethics as follows : ' The ideal of a Christian society as an end, and of the progressive realization of this ideal by an appropriate social practice, is an idea which in our day is in every one's mind. Now one would seek in vain for the slightest presentiment of such an idea in the mind of St. Thomas. For him, on the contrary, there are no Christian politics. He does not see that Christianity has inaugurated a new civilization. He does not even know that the Christian principles of right and justice are very different from those of antiquity, whether among the Gentiles or among the Jews. He knew, it is true, the great superiority of the new law to the old; he makes a comparison of the two laws, and shows that the new law is superior, in that it has as its end not any sensible and terrestrial good, but intelligible and celestial good, in that it regulates

4

not only outward actions but the movements of the mind, that it restrains the hand and the soul, in that it commands by love and not by fear. This is the reason of the superiority of the new law. But as for moral precepts, as for the regulation of outward actions and of the relations of men towards each other, the new law has made no innovations; it has had nothing to add to the old law. St. Thomas says this explicitly. " The new law had nothing to add to the old as regards external actions." And this ancient Jewish law was in his view, as far as morality is concerned, only the law of nature, the primitive law, so that in reality the moral law of humanity, according to St. Thomas, has not changed, and the morality of Christians does not differ from that of the ancients; at least it differs only in the order of grace, in what concerns the salvation of souls. But in the order of nature, for the precepts of justice, for the regulation of the relations of men to each other, and in consequence for the principles of politics, Christianity and antiquity have the same conscience.' I have quoted this because it shows clearly how little interested the most representative thinker of the middle ages was in the desire to Christianize social life by drawing out the implications of our Lord's teaching and applying them to new conditions. At the same time, I do not think that it is quite fair. It treats the law of nature as a concept which has always had the same content. This is not true. In the hands of Christian thinkers it has altered a good deal, and already in the time of St. Thomas was quite as much Christian as Stoical. Still, the complete absence of any conscious acceptance of evolution in morals is very striking, though even here we must remember that in the individual life he lays stress on the growth from nature to grace. For a genuinely evolutionary Catholicism we must wait for Tyrrell and his fellow Modernists, whose position has been formally condemned as incompatible with Catholic orthodoxy.

There was then still no programme of social reform in the middle ages, any more than in antiquity, though perhaps we may say that the reasons were not quite the same. For the early Church social reform was too difficult—the Church had not the power to make any great social or political changes. In the middle ages a programme of social reform would have seemed superfluous, since a harmony, so to speak, of the order of nature and the order of grace had already been established.

The difference between pre-Christian and Christian moral ideas is nevertheless greater than the schoolmen realized. Christ rejects all ethical systems which accept, as right and necessary, strife and warfare as conditions of social life; He lays very little stress on honour, pride, self-respect, and patriotism; for Him, love is the fulfilling of the law. In some ways, the conditions of life in late antiquity and the middle ages were not so unfavourable to this ideal as the gigantic modern State, with its rigorous demands upon the loyalty and self-sacrifice of its citizens, its swollen populations, and the inevitable struggle for existence which these conditions involve. At any rate, modern civilization confronts us with new problems, in which we could not have had much help from the mediaeval thinkers, even if they had shown any desire to look forward.

I have hurried over the mediaeval period because my space is restricted, and because I am probably right in supposing that you are most interested in the Gospels at one end of the story, and in modern conditions at the other.

But there is one generalization which I think may be safely made. The chief contributions to social reform on religious lines have been made, not by the great Churches, not by the Roman Catholics, nor the Anglicans, nor the Lutherans, but by the sects. We may think of the radical movements before the Reformation, usually stamped out with great cruelty; of the Anabaptists in the Reformation period, and the strange communistic outbreak at Münster; of the small sects in Cromwell's time, most of them with 'levelling' ideas; and of the Quakers, who, of all Christian bodies, have perhaps kept nearest to the real principles of the Gospel.

IV
THE SECT-TYPE OF CHRISTIANITY

IV
THE SECT-TYPE OF CHRISTIANITY

THE most distinctive feature of the Sect-type of Christianity, as compared with the Church-type, is the rejection of the double standard of morality which the Church had been driven to accept as a necessary concession. Life in the world, it was supposed, was necessarily life in a society where the state of sin compels men to acquiesce in much that is contrary to the law of God. Those who wish to be perfect are almost obliged to withdraw from society, and live the so-called religious life. There was a notion that God admitted a division of labour; the soldier might not have much time to pray, but the monk could pray for him. The merits of the saints might atone in part for the worldliness of secular life. This idea, which is capable of being expressed in a form which is by no means unreasonable, was thoroughly unacceptable to the sectaries. They believed that the Gospel was meant to be accepted in its entirety by everybody, and that the Church has no right to offer a much easier pass-examination to the majority. They repudiated the theory of works of supererogation and transferable merits; no man may deliver his brother or make agreement unto God for him.

The consequences of this were far-reaching. In the first place, the requirements of Christian morality were made more exacting. Some of the pleasures and enjoyments which the great Church had charitably tolerated among men and women living in the world, were now forbidden. A severer standard of living was set up for all who wished to be considered followers of Christ. But secondly, monkish asceticism, which obviously could not be demanded of the average family, was disparaged, and condemned as having no value. If it was not the duty of all, it could not be the duty of any. So the Catholic discipline was relaxed; and what was to be put in its place? Mere abstention from frivolous pleasures was not quite enough; the yoke of Christ must somehow be felt in the whole life. So a new kind of asceticism was encouraged. A man's calling might be made the occasion of his self-denial. For the first time in the history of Christianity, work, almost for its own sake, became treated as the typical service of God. Industry and thrift were exalted to a high place among the virtues, as they had been under the old Roman republic, but hardly since then.

This view of the Christian vocation, no longer as the life of meditation and spiritual detachment, but as steady devotion to some productive work useful to the community, was especially developed in Calvinism. From the practical point of view it worked almost too well. Calvinist societies have always become very prosperous, and have remained so until the religious basis of their prosperity has been undermined. The most salient instances are Scotland and the United States, where this type of business man has lingered on after the type has become almost extinct in England. It has been said that the successful man of business, if he is not a child of the Ghetto, is usually a grandchild of John Calvin.

Another consequence of the Sect-type of Christianity must be noted. What did the sectaries, who for the most part knew nothing of Aristotle, the Stoics, or the mediaeval schoolmen, make of the law of nature? Where did they find the law of nature? The answer is, they found it in the law of Christ, and in the decalogue, which by rather violent exegesis they so stretched as to make it cover nearly the whole duty of man. But the Sermon on the Mount was the main ethical authority. Now we have seen that the sectaries would have nothing to say to a double standard of ethics, and would not acquiesce in a separation of the ideal and the actual. The Sermon on the Mount was meant to be obeyed by all, and not only by individuals, but by a Christian State. For the first time, there was a stern demand that the law of the land should be brought into conformity with the law of nature, in other words, with the law of Christ. Here then, at last, we see the beginning of a development of Christian ethics which was implicit in the Church from the first, but which had hitherto remained quiescent. Christian ethics assumed a radical and even a revolutionary character. I may quote a manifesto of the Diggers in Cromwell's time, where, you will see, the appeal is made, not to the law of Christ, but to the absolute law of nature. 'First we demand, yea or no, whether the earth with her fruits was made to be bought and sold from one to another; and whether one part of mankind was made to be a lord of the land and another part a servant, by the law of creation before the fall?'

This, however, remained characteristic of some of the smaller sects; it was not true of the larger reformed Churches. The Anglican Church accepted the type of government set up in 1689; the recalcitrants, who were numerous, were chiefly adherents of the Stuarts, not political radicals. Lutheranism has generally supported the government; it has never been the organ of political disaffection; and Calvinism has, in practice, been in favour of democracy, but democracy of a very conservative type. In fact, the radical sects have not had much power or influence. They seemed to be about to come into their own under Cromwell; but their reign was a very short one.

The Lutheran Church has usually maintained a double standard of ethics, not, as in Catholicism, an 'honours' course for those who wish to be perfect, and a 'pass-degree' for the majority, but one standard for the individual, and another for the State. This, no doubt, in part goes back to the old distinction between the absolute law of nature and the relative law of nature, the latter being the necessary order under 'a state of sin'; but it has had the unfortunate consequence of accepting a purely selfish State-policy as justifiable under existing conditions. At the beginning of the Great War German theologians had accustomed their readers to the notion that Christian ethics are private and personal, and do not apply to international relations. The friends of peace everywhere recognize that disarmament and the abolition of war are impossible as long as this Machiavellian doctrine (which was supported without scruple by our own Francis Bacon) holds its own. The chief cause of modern wars is fear; and as long as governments think that they may further their own supposed interests without any reference to moral principle, these fears will be justified, and no nation will feel itself safe until it is stronger than any possible enemy, in which case its neighbours would have good grounds for believing themselves to be in danger. This exemption of governments and nations from the obligations of Christian morality has been one of the most disastrous blots upon modern civilization. In the middle ages the theory at least was less cynical.

The most interesting development of the new ideas of a Christian society is, I think, to be found in Quakerism, which was not distorted, as Lutheranism and Calvinism necessarily were, by the exigencies of politics. Quakerism is individualistic mysticism, a type of religion which might have played a much greater part in Church history if it had not been for the danger of internal disruption at a time when the Church was obliged to present a united front against her enemies. For the Quakers, Christ, the inner light, reason, the absolute law of nature, are all identical. It was hoped that if the rule of Christ could be set up on earth, all social evils, in particular war and the oppression of the poor, would disappear. Some kind of freewill Communism was in the minds of many—such an experiment as is described in the Acts of the Apostles as having been tried at

Jerusalem. But the basis was the Christian law of love; the sanctity of the family was not threatened; and above all, the use of force to bring about social amelioration was entirely abjured.

It was at this time that we find a resuscitation of Millenarianism, the expectation of a reign of the saints on earth, an age of assured social justice and happiness. It is very remarkable how this idea always tends to revive in certain states of the public mind. It was common in the primitive Church; Augustine says that he once believed it himself. It is the creation of ardent hopefulness. Religious people are never willing wholeheartedly to surrender either this world for the next or the next world for this; and Millenarianism is a kind of compromise. It is not obsolete by any means, though it has taken new forms. The secular religion of the nineteenth century was evolutionary Millenarianism, differing from the older forms only in anticipating a gradual instead of a catastrophic change. This was in accordance with the modern way of estimating historical events, and was a pseudo-scientific and quite illegitimate interpretation of Darwin's discoveries. Many Socialists seem to have reverted to catastrophic Millenarianism, in which, however, they do not look for divine assistance.

The ambition to bring secular institutions into

conformity with the law of Christ is a far more wholesome development of Protestantism than these Millenarian expectations, though we must remember that these latter are the creation of an optimistic temper, which is very favourable to getting something done, though the something is seldom what the optimist desired. But we ought to attribute great importance to those ' causes ' to which Evangelical Christians, and not least the Methodist Churches which sprang up in the eighteenth century, devoted themselves, in the hope of removing, one after another, the worst blots upon Christian civilization. These movements were a new thing. There were no ' causes ' in antiquity, nor in the middle ages, nor even in the early modern period. I have tried to show why this was so. In the early Church there was no power to carry social reforms; in the middle ages men thought it not worth while. So the record of the Church in the field of social reform was a poor one. It was not the Church which brought slavery to an end in Europe, or abolished torture, or condemned war. The Church was content to be like the ' Prayers ' in a famous passage of Homer, who hobble after the Demon of Infatuation (*Até*), lame and wrinkled and cross-eyed, and heal some of the damage which Até has done. Cure, not prevention, charity, not justice, was all that could be looked for from organized Christianity. But now a new type of crusader appeared. Devoted men and women, most of them belonging to the sects, or Free Churches as we now call them, devoted their lives to removing social abuses. Some agitated for the abolition of the slave-trade, and then for the abolition of slavery itself; others brought to light the cruelties practised in prisons and madhouses; others protested against the industrial exploitation of young children; others started a campaign against what was then a shameful national vice, drunkenness. The motive power in all these crusades was the conviction that in a Christian country social institutions ought to reflect the Christian consciousness; and further that in Christianizing these institutions and customs, they were acting in accordance with the immutable laws of God, that law of nature which was as old as creation itself.

The same conviction inspired the lives of a large number of honest and industrious business and professional people about this time. I have spoken of the peculiar form of asceticism which was developed in Protestantism, and especially where Calvinism was strong. The motive of industry was not gain, but the production of useful commodities, carried on as the work to which God has called us. Luxury-trades were not encouraged, and all dis-

5

honest handling of money, rigging markets, promoting bubble companies, adulteration and other tricks of trade, were forbidden to a Christian. The weak spot in this business ethics was the acceptance of work for its own sake as a virtuous occupation, without asking the question which Clough asks in one of his poems, though, in the spirit of his generation, he puts it by,

Go from the east to the west as the sun and stars direct thee,
Go with the girdle of man, go and encompass the earth,
Not for the gain of the gold, for the getting, the hoarding, the having,
But for the joy of the deed, but for the duty to do.
Go with the spiritual life, the higher volition and action,
With the great girdle of God go and encompass the earth.
Go; say not in thy heart, And what then, were it accomplished,
Were the wild impulse allayed, what were the use and the good?
Go; when the instinct is stilled, and when the deed is accomplished,
What thou hast done and shalt do shall be declared to thee then.

'What were the use and the good?' Alas, that is the question that the Puritan never asks. There was a fine idealism in his scheme of life, as Clough recognizes in these lines. He lived cleanly, he worked hard, he paid his way in the world and something more. He made Great Britain, for a time, the foremost nation in the world. But the civilization which he produced was ugly and irrational; as compared with France, England was hardly civilized. America is still ' a going concern,' on these lines; when we visit that country we can see, better even than at home, what Puritanism can do for a nation, and what it cannot do.

These reflections bring us down to our own time; and in dealing with the social duty of the Church to-day we can hardly escape being controversial. It is rather the custom now to disparage the social reformers of a hundred years ago—men like William Wilberforce—for not being sufficiently alive to the miseries of the poor at home. There is a mass of literature, of which the books by Mr. and Mrs. Hammond are a type, which, under an appearance of impartiality, are intended to excite our indignation against the industrial revolution and all its works. What, we are asked, was the Church doing in the generation before the Factory Acts? Why were the anti-slavery Nonconformists so tender only to men and women with black skins?

The conditions in the mines and factories were bad enough without being exaggerated. But let us remember this : we had to beat Napoleon, and we had to recover from the tremendous losses of the war. We did both; but we saved England for the remainder of the century by the rather grim labour conditions which we now condemn so virtuously. We talk of ' individualism ' as the crime of that age. But there is more individualism, more unwillingness to make sacrifices for the country now than there was then. The aggregate wealth of the country, it was thought, had to be augmented. The surplus was not squandered, but invested in new undertakings. The population went up by leaps and bounds—this being the work of the labouring class, who, it seems, did not feel the cruelty of child-labour so acutely as we do. Those of us who are old enough to remember England fifty or sixty years ago, must sigh for the days when Gladstone talked quite seriously of abolishing 'that inquisitional and unequal impost,' the income-tax; when the country was being run at a huge profit, and we were the envy of the world. I am not suggesting that the period of expansion could have been continued indefinitely in any circumstances, nor that we should wish for a state of things 'when wealth accumulates and men decay'—decay, I mean, not in numbers, but in physical and mental health. But I do ask you to consider, before you join in the popular declamations against the early Victorian age, the contrast between that period and the time in which we are living. We have got rid of what we are pleased to call individualism, and our politicians declare complacently that 'we are all Socialists now.' And we see our empire breaking up, our naval supremacy gone, our main industries rotting, our working population living on doles, and the sun of our prosperity manifestly sitting in cloud. What was the Church doing, not to bring about this happy state of things earlier? Well, perhaps it was minding its own business, though I hold no brief for the Anglican Church in Queen Victoria's reign.

The chief feature of Church history in Protestant countries and especially in England, during the last century, has been the secularizing of religion. For this there have been several causes. The great prosperity of the country turned away men's minds from spiritual things. The revival of mediaevalism in the Oxford Movement was a theory of the ministry rather than of the Church, and had little influence on the thought of the nation. Darwin's biology seemed at first to deny all teleology, and to favour the unchristian maxim, ' The devil take the hindmost.' It was also pressed into the service of the evolutionary Millenarianism already mentioned, and the idea of an inevitable and unending progress to perfection took strong hold of the imagination, driving out the pale phantom of belief in a future life. The Churches themselves were much to blame in presenting the doctrine of future rewards and punishments in such a crude and barbarous form that they aroused a moral as well as intellectual revolt. The heady wine of revolutionary propaganda also played its part.

The clergy found that if they preached from the text, ' If in this life only we have hope in Christ, we are of all men most miserable,' they were received with open derision. On the other hand they found some inclination on the part of the manual workers to accept Jesus Christ if He were disguised as a social agitator. Labour was ready to say, like Jacob, ' If the Lord will keep me in the way that I am going, and will give me food to eat and raiment to put on, then shall the Lord be my God.' Many of the parish priests and ministers, who worked among the masses, came to sympathize with their point of view. At the same time, some of the old dogmas of traditional theology were beginning to seem no longer credible. It was safer and easier for an ambitious preacher to specialize on temperance or education or housing.

For all these reasons, Christianity in the nineteenth century became a this-world religion, as it had never been before, and the clergy were more and more drawn into politics.

V

THE CHRISTIAN SOCIAL UNION

V

THE CHRISTIAN SOCIAL UNION

I HAVE no wish to underrate the deep moral earnestness of the men who in the last decade of the nineteenth century founded the 'Christian Social Union.' Bishop Gore thought that Christians who had seen the conditions of labour at first hand must have a 'permanently uneasy conscience.' If some of the abuses which aroused the indignation of these eloquent clergymen have now been mitigated, they should have their share of the credit. In order that my hearers may realize the manner in which they conducted their crusade, I will give, in an abbreviated form, extracts from a book which perhaps has now been almost forgotten, the volume of sermons called *Lombard Street in Lent* (Elliot Stock, 1894). But first I will give you a fiery exhortation from John Ruskin, who was undoubtedly one of the inspirers of the movement.

'If, on due and honest thought over these things, it seems that the kind of existence to which men are now summoned by every plea of pity and claim of right, may, for some time at least, not be a

luxurious one;—consider whether, even supposing
it guiltless, luxury would be desired by any of us
if we saw clearly at our sides the suffering which
accompanies it in the world.	Luxury is, indeed,
possible in the future; luxury for all and by the
help of all; but luxury at present can only be
enjoyed by the ignorant; the cruellest man living
could not sit at his feast unless he sat blindfold.
Raise the veil boldly; face the light; and if as yet
the light of the eye can only be through tears, and
the light of the body through sackcloth, go thou
forth weeping, bearing precious seed, until the time
come, and the kingdom, when Christ's gift of
bread and bequest of peace shall be " Unto this last
as unto thee." '

In the book of sermons referred to, Canon Scott
Holland points out that a Joint Stock Company has
no conscience.	No one knows with whom the
responsibility lies.	Now and again the shareholder
finds that he has reaped profit from some course of
action which has sweated down some miserable
workers into infamous conditions of toil and life;
or has made home life impossible for them through
the long hours that we have imposed upon them;
or has poisoned them through neglect of the pre-
cautions which should have been made imperative;
or we have got rents from slums which were a
sanitary disgrace and a moral degradation; or

from public houses which fatten on hideous drunkenness.

How inhuman, too, is commercial speculation! It takes advantage of others' ignorance, stupidity, and infirmities; its normal work exaggerates all disturbances and fluctuations of the money market. It stamps down what shows signs of weakness, so that recovery is made impossible; it runs up anything that promises well into unhealthy and inflated pre-eminence, and then hastily deserts it before the recoil follows which its own exertions have made inevitable.

So he calls the nation to collective penitence.

Another preacher, taking for his text ' Am I my brother's keeper?' quotes some fine lines from James Russell Lowell.

> Said Christ our Lord, I will go and see
> How the men, My brethren, believe in Me.
>
> .   .   .   .   .
>
> Great organs surged through arches dim,
> Their jubilant floods in praise of Him;
> And in church and palace and judgement hall
> He saw His image high over all.
> But still, wherever His steps they led,
> The Lord in sorrow bent down His head;
> And from under the heavy foundation stones
> The Son of Mary heard bitter groans.
> Have ye founded your thrones and your altars then
> On the bodies and souls of living men?
> And think ye that building shall endure
> Which shelters the noble and crushes the poor?
>
> .   .   .   .   .

Then Christ sought out an artisan,
A low-browed, stunted, haggard man,
And a motherless girl, whose fingers slim
Pushed from her family want and sin.
These led He in the midst of them,
And as they drew back their garments' hem
For fear of defilement, Lo here, said He,
The images ye have made of Me.

Christ will say to the callous and the slothful, with such a glance as struck Gehazi with leprosy and Simon Magus with a curse, 'What hast thou done? Smooth religionist, orthodox Churchman, phylacterized Pharisee, thy brother's blood crieth unto Me from the ground.' Men triumphantly quote the words of Deuteronomy, 'The poor shall never cease out of the land,' and forget the words which follow, 'Therefore I command thee saying, Thou shalt surely open thy hand to thy brother, to thy needy, and to thy poor in the land. Thou shalt surely give to him, and thy heart shall not be grieved when thou givest to him, because for this thing the Lord shall bless thee in all thy works.'

'Many a man in his affection and service to his family forgets that he belongs also to the collective being; that he cannot without guilt sever himself from the needs of his parish, his nation, and his race.

'There is but one test with God of membership of the kingdom of heaven. "He that doeth righteousness is righteous, and is born of God."'

A third preacher urges that property, which is the product of the whole society except the idlers, is ultimately subject to the control of the State. Property is indefensible, except on condition that it renders service to the community.

Quoting the parable of the rich fool, he says: The first peril of the rich man is the inordinate desire of accumulation. Avarice means eagerness for gain beyond the limit necessary to a man's station in life. To hoard or amass money beyond limit for private ends is, in a sense, to steal it, for wealth is a social good. A second peril is selfishness in expenditure. Property is not sacred in the sense that a man may do what he wills with his own. A third peril is in the paralyzing of moral and spiritual effort. ' Take thine ease, eat, drink, and be merry.' ' Woe unto you that are rich, for ye have received your consolation.' Luxury tends gradually to deaden the soul, to kill out high aspirations, to form a crust about us which the call to social service cannot pierce.

The prophets warned the ancient world what a corrupt society must expect—a society that refused to be reformed. ' Woe to the oppressing city, for the just Lord is in the midst thereof.' ' Woe to them that are at ease in Zion.'

The Gospel plainly teaches, first, that wealth is not the true end of man. ' A man's life consisteth not in the abundance of the things that he possesseth.' He quotes an American writer, A. D. White: 'The greatest work which the coming century has to do is to build up an aristocracy of thought and feeling which shall hold its own against the aristocracy of mercantilism.' The mercantile spirit has created a class of men in whom all the finer traits of character are extinguished; whose aspirations are dwarfed, whose sympathies are destroyed; men benumbed in conscience, brutalized in feeling, whose right is might, and who know no law but the law of their own audacity. It is the first principle of Christianity that a man's worth is to be estimated not by what he has but by what he is. Secondly, the Gospel says that wealth must be *justly* acquired. A man is bound to ask himself, How have I become rich? Has he given a fair equivalent? Has he made money at the expense of the spiritual and bodily lives of others? Has he grown rich by fraud and false pretences? Does he own shares in a company which issues lying advertisements, and recognizes no responsibility for the welfare of its employees? Such reflections may awaken our consciences. Thirdly, the Gospel teaches the duty of *moderation*. It is the want of moderation in acquisition which is mainly respons- ible for the class of irreconcilables, who wish to wreck everything.

Then there is the responsibility for *use*. Prof. Marshall has said that 'more than half of the consumption of the upper classes of society in England is unnecessary.' Mr. Lilly says: 'The only things which a man can, in strictness, call his own—and even here he is under the law of conscience—are his spiritual, intellectual, and physical faculties. Of the material surroundings which he calls "mine," he is but a usufructuary, a trustee. The entire accumulated wealth of the country, natural and fabricated, is in the last resort the property of the country.' Finally the preacher quotes from Robertson of Brighton: 'To the spirit of the Cross alone we look as the remedy for social evils. When the people of this country, especially the rich, shall have been touched with the spirit of the Cross to a largeness of sacrifice of which they have not dreamed as yet, there will be an atonement between the rights of labour and the rights of property.'

Another preacher, taking as his subject commercial morality, gives some very telling quotations from the answers given by business men to a questionnaire about the possibility of observing a high standard of integrity in business. The answers for the most part confirm the severe judgement of Herbert Spencer: 'It has been said that the law of the animal creation is, Eat and be eaten; and of our trading community it may similarly be said that the law is, Cheat and be cheated. A system of keen competition, carried on as it is without adequate moral restraint, is very much a system of commercial cannibalism. Its alternatives are, Use the same weapons as your antagonist, or be conquered and devoured.'

Two employers wrote : ' Business is based on the gladiatorial theory of existence. If Christian truth and justice is not consistent with this, business is in a bad case. So is nature.'

Two others answer : 'Not only difficult but impossible. For a man is not master of himself. If one would live and avoid the bankruptcy court, one must do business on the same lines as others do, without troubling whether the methods are in harmony with the principles of Christian truth and justice or not.'

The preacher mentions three practices which ' appear to be absolutely wrong '—adulteration of goods which cannot be known to the buyer; false statements as to the history and quality of goods; commissions, when given as bribes for breaches of trust. He quotes, ' Putting away lying, speak every man truth to his neighbour, for we are members one of another.' If, he says, the game could be played fairly, with some regard for simple truth and common honesty, the existing system would appear much more tolerable.

At this point, even the most convinced opponent of socialistic schemes will probably realize the strength of the indictment against competitive industrialism. Here we have honourable, or would-be honourable business men confessing that if they tried to do business honestly they would certainly be bankrupt; that honesty is assuredly not the best policy now; that there is no such thing as honest trade, and that nearly all fortunes are made by what Roman law would call force (*vis*) or fraud. If this is true, what becomes of the theory that private ownership is part of the law of nature?

It is rather interesting to remember that the early Quakers forbade bargaining. Every Quaker shopkeeper marked his goods with the lowest price that he would accept. This is the rule now in highly industrialized nations, but it was almost unheard of then. The result was that almost everybody went to the Quaker shops, since most people do not wish to ' do,' they only want not to be ' done.' It seems possible that attempts to moralize business might not be so hopeless as they appear.

As a practical application of this principle, the Christian Social Union at Oxford made inquiries about different firms, and published lists of trades-men whom they considered to be just to their work-

6

men and fair to their customers. This generally
meant a tacit boycotting of firms which paid less
than the standard rate of wages. The experiment
was not long continued.

I will quote from one more sermon by a member
of this group—about women's work forty years ago.
We must entirely sympathize with the speaker.
'Look at that young girl in the drapery establish-
ment. You look in early in the morning—there she
is, standing and arranging the goods, after lifting
down heavy weights quite beyond her strength. In
the afternoon, still in the same position; at six, still
standing; at eight-thirty still standing; on Satur-
day at nine, ten, eleven, still standing; and then
look at her anaemic face, and ask yourself what is
the real reason that allows such conditions to be in
force? And so I might take you through factory
and restaurant, through laundry and white-lead
works, and into the homes of our home workers, at
eleven, twelve, and one at night. I could read you
pages of evidence revealing the circumstances
under which our women work, where nothing is
done except by compulsion; where every advantage
is taken of the weakness of women; where ordinary
decency is impossible; and where all the instincts
of womanhood are crushed,'

VI
GENERAL CONCLUSIONS

VI
GENERAL CONCLUSIONS

It is notoriously difficult to draw the line between moral and political reforms. But on the whole I agree with what Harnack said on the subject twenty-five years ago. ' The vast apparatus of the Church has a right to exist only if it renders real service to the whole body—not by words, but by evangelical and social work, work in which every order must perform its own share. But the more stress is laid on this, the more need there is to define the limits within which the Church must confine its activity—bounds that do not include economic questions. It has nothing to do with such practical questions of social economics as the nationalization of private property and enterprise, land-tenure reforms, restriction of the legal hours of work, price-regulations, taxation, and insurance; for in order to settle these matters, such technical knowledge is required as is altogether outside the province of the Church, and if it were to meddle with them at all it would be led into a secularization of the worst description. But it is its duty to interfere in public conditions wherever it finds that serious moral evils are being tolerated. Can it be right for the Church, as it were, to shrug its shoulders and pass prostitution by in silence, as the priest did the man who had fallen among thieves? Is it enough to collect money for penitentiaries, leaving it to particular Christian associations to fight against the evil? Dare it again keep silence when it sees a state of things destructive of the sanctity of marriage and of family life, and devoid of the most elementary conditions of morality? Dare it look calmly on while the weak are trodden under foot, and none lends a helping hand to people in distress? Dare it hear without rebuking it, language which, in the name of Christianity, destroys the peace of the land and throws scorn and hatred broadcast? Is it not the duty of an institutional Church to preserve peace, both civil and international, to draw together rich and poor, and help to break down mischievous class prejudices? Besides this, there are many important tasks which Christians cannot regard with indifference, although their accomplishment lies outside the actual scope of the Church. Purely economic questions must admittedly be estimated and decided only from an economic standpoint; but there are many which affect vitally the moral condition of the people. Therefore the Church must not obstruct the discussion of such subjects among its members, for it is to the interest of the whole Church that warm-hearted, clear-sighted Christians should so study the subject as to be able to distinguish those efforts at reform which are full of promise for the future from such as are merely visionary. . . . It cannot be denied that the whole history of the Church shows that when warm-hearted Christians take up economic questions, they tend to favour radical projects. . . . Even Protestantism is not free from the danger that some day a second Arnold of Brescia may appear, and clerical students of political economy attempt in the name of the Gospel to prescribe to others the attitude which, if they are to retain the name of Christians, they must assume towards social questions. It is a more than questionable procedure to condemn " the rich," and whole classes of the nation, and dream that it will be possible, by beginning at the bottom, to construct an entirely new Christian commonwealth. These are only passing indications of what might happen in the future; but things have their own logic, and those who have sown the wind will reap the whirlwind.'

Putting Harnack's argument in my own words, I should say that every citizen has a duty to try to form an intelligent opinion on social questions, and a right to express that opinion and to persuade others to adopt it. This applies to ministers of religion no less than to laymen. But, as Harnack says, a warm-hearted Christian needs to be on his guard to prevent his heart running away with his head. Most of the problems which, in their entirety, we call the social question, are extremely complex, and cannot be decided off-hand on sentimental grounds. For example, war is a gigantic evil, and probably an unnecessary evil. It may have been inevitable at one time, but not now. Nevertheless, the causes of it have their roots deep in human nature and in the structure of society. Mere denunciation cannot do much good. The Churches may give their whole-hearted support to the League of Nations, because it is certain that the objects of the League are such as Christ would approve. Here is a case where quasi-political action on the part of the Church is justified. Nor can there be any reasonable doubt that the Churches were right in following the lead of Rome in protesting against the horrible and blasphemous persecution of religion in Russia. But when we come to such questions as outdoor relief and housing, the case is by no means so clear. There is a danger that ill-considered remedies may aggravate the evil which they are meant to cure. To withdraw large sums of money from private and voluntary expenditure may destroy confidence and increase unemployment. These are not questions which ministers of religion are specially qualified to answer, and the shallow rhetoric in which they are prone to indulge does not tend to clarify the issue. Nor have groups of clergymen any right to invoke the authority of Christ, or of the Church, to decide questions on which good men notoriously differ.

There is a very great temptation for a religious body to organize itself so strictly that it can command a calculable number of votes. These it promises to a political party which will support some ecclesiastical interest, or will pledge itself to oppose some measure which it dislikes. In this way a Church may wield political power out of all proportion to its numbers. The Church of Rome adopts this policy without any reserve, and has unquestionably been able to prevent a few measures which commend themselves to the judgement of the majority. But this is the way to rot democracy; it is utterly and entirely wrong. And yet even here there may be some doubtful cases. If the State wished to make marriages terminable by mutual consent, would it or would it not be legitimate for the Church to say to a candidate, ' Unless you pledge yourself to vote against this measure, we shall turn you out ' ? Some of you will no doubt remember how, in Gladstone's time, the Noncon-formists supported him with such energy that their chapels were almost turned into Liberal committee-rooms at a General Election. Personally I think Gladstone was more often right than wrong; but I have no doubt that this close association of the Free Churches with one political party has, on the whole, diminished their religious influence. There is a group of Radical Anglicans who are evidently attracted by the same policy. I do not in the least object to their making speeches and printing pamphlets in support of socialist legislation, but they have no right to invoke the authority of Christ or of the Church.

In conclusion, I will try to make rather clearer what, in my opinion, the attitude of the Church ought to be towards schemes for the better organization of society. I have said quite frankly that in the New Testament we do not find the guidance that we should desire, because the idea of a Christianized world, advancing by degrees towards a social order under which the kingdom of God might be realized on earth, is quite foreign to the earliest Christians, and remained foreign to the Catholic Church until very recent times. For us, modern science has opened out an entirely new perspective. Instead of the cramped cosmography and history of past ages, we are encouraged to see before us an almost boundless vista of time during which the human race may realize all its possibilities. The past of civilization has filled some ten thousand years; the future may last for a hundred thousand or even a million. We are still children; we have, as a race, nearly all our life before us. This new vista has altered, and ought to alter, our whole way of looking at the world. We have no freehold here; but a lease of 999 years is, I believe, practically the same as a freehold. Such thoughts make us realize, as we never could before, the splendid adventure of the life of our race as a whole; its glorious possibilities; the unimportance of temporary failures; and the privilege which we enjoy of being links in so magnificent a chain. A new range of duties springs into view—all our duties to posterity. We include in our moral scheme the duty of safeguarding the resources and the threatened beauties of our home, and our distant cousins the lower animals, which, if they are once exterminated, are gone for ever. Still more, the young science of eugenics is seen to concern us deeply. 'Keep the young generations in hail, and bequeath them no tumbled house.'

Yes, this earth of ours has become more precious to us, and we may people it in imagination with a race of human beings far superior in every way to us and our contemporaries. And yet we must repeat what we said at the beginning of this Lecture. The Gospel is a message of moral and spiritual regeneration, not of social reform. As

Christians, our business is with the inside, not the outside, of the cup, with the building up of character, not with the improvement of external conditions.

Do we really think that the work assigned to us as Christians is less important than that which occupies the attention of politicians? Do we really think that any solid and stable amelioration of society can be made without a new heart and a new spirit? If we do, we shall be making a far worse mistake than the early Church did when it neglected social reform altogether. For the mind of Christ was kept alive in the cloisters and in the sacraments of the Catholic Church. But an externalized and secularized Christianity has neither savour nor salt; it has no dynamic to regenerate the world.

However long may be our lease of our present home; however splendid may be the possibilities which applied science seems to promise us, this earth is but the shadow of heaven, an imperfect copy of the eternal and spiritual world which surrounds us and penetrates us, closer than breathing and nearer than hands and feet, but invisible and impalpable. There, in the eternal world, is the home of the ultimate values—Goodness, Truth, and Beauty—which give to our visible world all of worth that it possesses; there is our heart's true home; there is the presence of

God. Against this spiritual world, as a background, is set all that we admire and love here on earth. And so, with all our enthusiasm for making life a better and happier thing for our brethren, we must never forget the words of St. Paul, 'We look not at the things that are seen, but at the things that are not seen. For the things that are seen are temporal; the things that are not seen are eternal.'